Evidence of Things Seen

Evidence of Things Seen

Richard Wollman

THE SHEEP MEADOW PRESS
RIVERDALE-ON-HUDSON, NY

All inquiries and permission requests should be addressed to:
The Sheep Meadow Press
P.O. Box 1345
Riverdale-on-Hudson, NY 10471

Designed and typeset by The Sheep Meadow Press.
Distributed by The University Press of New England.

Printed on acid-free paper in the United States. This book meets the guidelines for permanence and durability of the Committee on Production Guidelines for Book Longevity of the Council on Library Resources.

Library of Congress Cataloging-in-Publication Data

Evidence of things seen / Richard Wollman.
p. cm.
Includes bibliographical references.
ISBN 1-931357-30-7 (alk. paper)
I. Title.

PS3623.O593E95 2006
811'.6--dc22

Acknowledgments

I wish to thank the editors of the following journals in which versions of these poems, some with different titles, first appeared:

American Literary Review: The Poet, Job; Self-Portrait
Americas Review: Prayer
Arion: Mythology
Bellevue Literary Review: And in Spring, Memoria
The Comstock Review: Spies, The Lamps
Crazyhorse: All in the Mind, Better Light
Florida Review: Catch & Release
Gulf Coast: Relativity in America, 1936
MARGIE: 1943
Meridian: Letter to Prague, 1948
New Delta Review: The View
New England Review: Paper in Autumn
Notre Dame Review: Association for the Recovery of Historical Memory, Conversion, The Gardener, The Rabbis, Remembrance
Prairie Schooner: Le Ghetto, Need, The Wild Corbières
Salamander: Lester Young in Paris, Pressure, Transport
Seattle Review: To Django Reinhardt
Smartish Pace: The Blue Men of Provence
The Sow's Ear Poetry Review: The Bioluminescent Bay
Tar River Poetry: No Better Claim

"Relativity in America, 1936" was awarded the 2005 *Gulf Coast* Prize.

"All in the Mind" was the featured poem at *Poetry Daily*, 6/28/04.

"A Cemetery Affair," "To Django Reinhardt," "The Lamps," "No Better Claim," and "Spies" are published on the Campbell Corner Poetry website.

"Le Ghetto" was reprinted in *Simmons Review* (2004).

"A Cemetery Affair" and "Evidence of Things Unseen" are reprinted in *The Powow River Poets Anthology* (Ocean Publishing, 2006).

Versions of some of these poems appear in a chapbook, *A Cemetery Affair* (Finishing Line Press, 2004).

My heartfelt thanks to Sean Singer, Carol Frost, Afaa Michael Weaver, and Edward Tayler for the benefit of their wisdom and expertise. I am grateful for the support I received from Albert Goldbarth, Dave Smith, Stanley Moss, Alfred Nicol, Len Krisak, Adrienne Wollman, Rhina Espaillat, and the Powow River Poets. My thanks to Simmons College for an Annual Fund for Research grant and a Bravo Award.

for my father

There must be in the world about us
things that solace us quite as fully as any
heavenly visitation would.

Wallace Stevens

The thing seen becomes the thing unseen.

Wallace Stevens

CONTENTS

I.

II.

III.

I.

Mythology

When Orion moves in December
just outside the mudroom
I lose interest

in the moon, which hangs there
and cannot compare
with the strong belt of stars,
the broad sword suspended,

though what gets me more
are his arms and legs extended,
splayed not like a hunter,
more like the hunted,

whose likeness to his prey
is seen by any eyes that know
our oldest witness.

Paper in Autumn

For the Salzer family

Each time the brigands arrived to herd them
onto the airless trains,

to Terezin, Zilina, finally to Poland,
Armin fled to the grove.

No camp could contain him, not until
he met that woman from Trencin
who gave him a beautiful boy.

Then the wood lost its hold on him,
his anonymity gone,

the trees turned to paper, yellowing
before his eyes,

all of them inscribed with his name, rooted
in the certainty of the earth.

He tried to bury himself in the grass,
to rub the sweet, dark dirt on his skin.

★

Our family was fed to an open fire.

Armin left the grove in autumn
to join the transport with his wife and his child:

the sweet smell of her skin captured him,
the boy's soft hair.

4

I tell you, he was the only one whose death
was not witnessed.

We wait for news. No one believed
the flames would reach him.
Nothing was written.

Transport

A golden calf dangled on a chain between her breasts.
The glory in such ornament was sex,
the song stripped of allegory.

Bless God and die, die in her arms, a voice sang,
and I saw her face in the light the wooden slats let in.

Outside, a boy was waving
as he admired the streaming engine.

The woman, for all her charms, was not strange.
Be like a gazelle, she said, and I leapt
from the train.

I climbed the imageless rock,
found a cleft fragrant with sage,
and there I took no rest.

Relativity in America, 1936

In Europe, Einstein needed to think fast
to keep things from occurring
at the same time.

It was a universal now
he wanted to prevent. Why not
give to each his own time and fiction
to stave off death?

Hadn't signals been embedded
in the Vienna evening?

Der Nachtfalter:
a nightclub's flashing light.

Three German youths descended on Gödel,
the blows cascading on his head,
pounding the time into him,
fixing him in place.

He was a moth
navigating the false signals of the moon
only to flit against an ordinary light
in America,

welcoming eternity in a small room
with no distinction of tenses.

He began to walk. He walked with Einstein
muttering of the universe
in eternal German.

Were they walking westward
to meet their younger selves?—

two signals flashing back and forth,
where they were glad and the world was
all before them.

Remembrance

Forsythia spills over fences
in Connecticut:
               the rest remains bare.
Survivors light candles, sulphur
from the match curling
               around their heads.
A cantor sings Kaddish as much for the living
               as the dead.
We have put on our good clothes.
We have driven through the pleasant country
               to take our seats on a stage.
I listen to the audience: am I someone
singing to himself
               to make silence less?
Or rouse a voice where there is none,
and, nothing myself, resurrect
               the living from the dead.

Lester Young in Paris

Pres heard in Debussy the strains of be-bop.
The sevenths. Thirteenths. Flatted fifths.

In the studio he wore felt slippers.
It was a way to live,

deaden the noise of fists,
the reedy wheeze of his breath

stolen one night in a white barracks.
And the squawk of hospital doors up north.

In curved brass, pain takes
the shape of song, the sense

variously drawn out. What can be made
of the low sounds

of men? He drank deep
until he finally drowned them.

To Django Reinhardt

Night found us in Apt
hurrying down alleys, listening
for Django, doubting we'd find him
so far from the Hot Club,
the streets as deserted as during the Occupation
when jazz was forbidden
and the crippled fingers of his chord hand
still played. Now we're lost, mistaken
about the place. Floodlights come on.
A courtyard door opens to a quartet
playing *Django's Dream*. Above the crowd
a boy leaps, his mattress hidden below the window.
When he sees us watching him
his thin body disappears.

Time in Provence

I. Bonnieux

North from Marseille an uncertain road
winds through a cleft in the Luberons.
Voices rise and fall and fade
with the landscape. We see faces
silhouetted against the backdrop
of stone houses, their silence relentless
as the time of day when doors close
and no one walks in the shuttered square.
No one knows of the house we need to find.
We have to make our way at dusk, turning
a key in different gates until one opens,
and we climb seven terraces, brush webs
from our faces, our eyes useless. We trip
darkly over apples falling on the path.

II. Pernes-les-Fontaines

We walk through a maze of stone and water
and find a fountain, a cherub
hovering near a garden
littered with fruit we can't identify.

Our son won't eat anything but olive after olive.
We don't know why it isn't pleasant,
why we are so silent.

Maybe it's the two boys circling the gate
before deciding to come in. For no reason
they crush their cigarettes, begin circling again,
sure, somehow, that we are not what we seem.

They disappear as the gate rattles
and a woman comes near, near enough
to see black hair cut close to her head,
her grey teeth, her age impossible to tell.

She had seen us from a window,
found at last the fruit she was looking for,
and was hurrying down to bring it for the boy.

III. Avignon

Women dressed as clowns in the piazza,
giving out apples.

Near the carousel the wind took up a woman's dress
as she looked at the Pope's palace.

I gave a five-franc note to the pale girl
who kept the children secure.

I said, *It's for the way you take care of them.*

She said, *No, I couldn't,* but I held her hand
until the note disappeared.

She could give it to herself later when she left
to unwind after the hours of turning,

the apples falling, the papers blowing
around the square.

The sky drifted behind a stream of banners
cascading down the walls of the museum

where a red virgin gazed
into a blue child's eyes.

Memoria

Robert Wallach, 1961-1968

I used to see when I looked at you,
two halves, mirrored images—
now I can't fathom where you are
except at night, cold
while I dream of your hands,
their delicately-lined translucent veins
a blue light I can't touch.

I started toward you once.
It was snowing.
I was a snow man looking out the window
at the garden's thickening limbs.
I heard myself say, *Take me*
to the place between our yards
where I never stopped throwing
a baseball at a pitch-back
for all the hours you left to me.

You lay in a hospital bed.
I lurked in the schoolyard,
picked fights with boys, taunted them
to feel their tight knuckles pummeling me
until someone would come to end it.

When someone was sent to say you were dead,
I had already known
because of the quiet outside, the stillness,
the leaves' refusal to harbor the breeze
as the hum of the heat bugs increased.

A lamp burned in your kitchen at night.
I saw your parents and mine, watched them try
to stop themselves from going to sleep,
already beginning to forget
the smallness of your hands.
How quickly you became your objects,
your bicycle, baseball cards I kept
as a hedge against my decaying memory.

★

So I think until my own son is born,
his furious heart pumping, his face red,
his lung collapsed like a bag as he struggles
for air. A faint sound leaves his mouth,
chest leaping up, his face my face.
A blizzard of nurses shoves me aside,
takes him to an oxygen tent. A voice says,
Do you think he has my hands?

Lines slip from the pulsing monitors
that count his breaths. We'll need to keep him,
someone says, while I think,
See how he calms himself hour by hour?
I pretend my hand repairs his loss of air,
and he sees me holding him,
and the tubes slide away,
the machines finally quiet as he breathes,
and we leave that place without looking back.

On the eighth day my father holds the baby's legs
near a knife. My son sees himself in the reflection.

And in Spring

Time beats with a constant pulse, and pain
in my legs does its best to find new ways
for me to notice, though now there is
a slight lift in the air, the cold the same
as before but with somewhere else to go
as the mud weather comes.

Here by the river hopeful people count
alewives swimming upstream to spawn.
When I try to wake my son,
I see how his legs have grown lean
disappearing into a blanket like twin fish
as the morning flashes under the current.

All in the Mind

On the day to buy the pumpkins,
children wearing masks
pressed their faces against the glass
of an orange bus.

            You could imagine
how you would pick her up, point
to where the birds were circling, ready to show her
how chaos becomes a silver arrow, then leaves.

You've dreamt it. The kid off in Europe,
barefoot in the fountains,
a Roman boy buying her coffee,
touching her later in her room.

            This is when you wish
you could call God back to say it was by design
that you never had this child, that you could
keep her here and hold her in the mind.

The Wild Corbières

A girl, yellow hair streaked with black,
screams as people pass.

She is not the genie of the empty fountain
where she sits, no siren of the village.

She does not know what she needs
to be unsatisfied,

having gazed so long the mountains disappear
and the light leads nowhere.

First there must be something to compare,
something ordinary that is and is not real—

not the église—no ringing repetitions
that fail utterly to alter the air.

Until then she sounds in broken notes
dissatisfaction with what isn't there.

Winter Confession: New England

At a plain table in an attic room
I sit, pure as a Cathar in perfection;

free from the matter of this earth,
the smell of moss, of humus, of dirt,

he makes ablutions, the body lost
to the thought of drawing itself near
its better version.

For this, priests unleashed inquisitors
in Beziers, in Carcassone,

where they devised a bloodless method.
I confess—I did not know my neighbor.

I kept to myself, rarely leaving my garden;
he smoked long cigars alone in upstairs rooms.

I would see him tending the spindly arms
of what was left

of his rows of roses.
(They were his wife's, I was told,
who died years ago.)

Once I saw him take an axe to the ice
hooding the steps to his door.

I had not known what purity there is
in mourning.

The Condition of Music

Why sing of the great dark eyelids of Lester Young?

Why yearn for the slurred speech of his sax
dragging up syllables

                           rolling words into notes
to make them well again?

The evening's dross slipped from a spit-hole.
What was human in the song.

If we finally turned to see the sound
it would be a stay

of execution, glorious sun
burning away cool perspiration

after fever-break, reprieve
from words we would have to use again

                         in the terrible blown night.

II.

Wedding Songs

For the poet, Sean Singer

I.
The glass breaks, and the women are dancing—:
in a ring the women dance,
                              mesmerizing men.

A chair is lifted on a spiral of notes
sprung from an unrepentant clarinet.

It floats on a klezmer wave of blue-black pain
rising to the heavens, seeding clouds with song

that returns as rain to help us bear
what cannot be named,

how Singer's fingers grip the chair to keep joy
from carrying him away.

II.
Surrounded by the women, Singer
and his bride ascend the stairs,
steep where they turn

toward a room prepared for them,
faint music clinging to their skin,
having become the world's

                              dark microcosm,
which Singer will come to know
as God's bright shadow.

Singer thinks God does not listen to him
singing from his own book of life.

III.
His bride's fledgling congregation
rents the basement of a church—:
the synagogue is deaf to their praying.

        In Florida, Singer sees
survivors walk sweltering streets,
nearly homeless, almost dead. Who will sing

of their dissipation, their naked arms,
their uncovered heads? The sun
illuminates the Memorial to the Dead

where Singer, feeding words to pigeons,
dreams of liberation. His hands are shaking.

It is the joy in Singer. It is joy
that makes me say, Amen,
        and again, Amen.

The Poet, Job

What is there to make of ashes? he thought.
They vanished in his swollen hands.
Wasn't it the breathing of his young son
he heard? Was it his wife? Still near?
Not even an animal's braying stirred
                              the stolid air.
Dry syllables. Dust. Chokewords.
The sound of his voice he could not bear.
A prayer echoed until it burst. A flood,
                    a whirlpool turning.
Let him curse the eyelids of the morning,
darken stars, forget his own birth. Nothing
comes of nothing. What else was left to him
but to put out the lights?
                        His choice to make
as God withdrew, became his silence,
a cloud's bright voltage or pillar of smoke.
The poet placed his hand over his mouth.

Signs of Devotion

I. Kabbalists

The sun descended in Arles,
its imprint on the moon a yellow memory
on the evening's thin cloth.

The night changed the view
as if its mind had been elsewhere.

The stars did not so much as blink
as they looked down on Mont Ventoux.

Meanwhile a blind rabbi
instructed kabbalists in a room
to write nothing others could construe,

content as he was with the spheres
under his palms as the stars
began to wheel and sing.

And the women came in
to place food where they sat
together at the evening's table.

II. Sun and Moon

A full eclipse began to leave
crescents on the complacent path.

Tourists and townspeople alike
were wearing cardboard safety glasses.

For once everyone was looking up.

At the top of the village, the church
obstructed the view.

The bakery had closed its doors.
There was no one left to catch
the aroma of the Sunday bread.

A bearded man eyed the people,
the little light that was left
making him squint.

His mouth opened but no words came.
He touched the number on his skin.

He spit in the dirt at the illusion
as the sun masqueraded as the moon.

III. The Mistral

When the wind takes hold of the streets
in Provence, it lashes the shuttered houses.
In the difficult light,
blue cypresses bend toward mountains
that are stone ramparts of themselves.
It moves the people inside
to muted rooms where they gaze
within the memory at their open windows.
This is the only sign of their devotion,
the province of olive-green thoughts
felt in the wind's steadfast buffeting.
As the Jews faded into the west
they did not take God with them
but followed as he withdrew
swirling around Spanish minarets,
fleeing vineyards of churned rock
where the self needs no companion.

Need

I.

In Feuilla, the iron key
to the église is hidden
underneath a loose stone.

II.

Look: the white rock of Leucate,
the garrigue along the road,
the sage green olive leaves
all wait for nothing.

The mountains give
their shape to the air
and do not find
the wind difficult.

Only Narcissus would think
there is no yearning
for some brief rain
here at the summer's zenith

so close to the sea.

III.

Christ in the countryside
finds his niche in the trees.

Where the wood meets wood he sleeps,
his back to the église.

His olive face rests
on a milk-white arm

as yellow light moves
from time to time

without wondering
what people need.

IV.

The fog down from the mountain
dampens the voices of evening swimmers,
hundreds losing themselves
where white surf meets the white mist.

The sky and the mountain are gone, and the sea
becomes itself in its own midst;
the only place to be known is in the sand,
the desert of the beach.

Light gives way to the violet night.
The procession begins: people walk
with the same slow step, heads bowed,
saying nothing, reaching for each other's hands.

1943

The slap of wings, pigeon's eyes
aimed at no one. Nothing personal
in the sky,

            the day's ashes
serenely floating

from the camps just forty miles away,
far as a still life with pineapples
resting on a table in Hartford.

Along the city's fences, Russians
and big-boned Polish girls trade
the more precious,

            the currency of hands
hawking bits of chocolate,
a shirt whose reworked seams
might hold until spring.

            One must live—
or not, as much for a potato,
a blessing of melted snow,
anything that bears enough
of the real: the red pain of the wind
quickening the blood.

Conversion

At the back of the cathedral, the Jews stood
under a stone globe carved with swarming rats.

A hand glided over them,
they relinquished their names,
became echoes,

footfall on cold marble, the plash
of unearthly water.

The late sun shone in the stained glass
of their skin, in the cardinal's vestments.

Incense curled over polished pews——:
where they looked they saw
only images.

Better Light

The light was in and out of the clouds
then nudged away for good. Was it nighttime?
My son was confused.

                    My mother called
on a cell phone wanting to describe
a sunset the color of Florida.

A dull urge made me go outside
to hack and hack away
at a defenseless shrub—

                    I'd thought to shape it,
make it round again. The branches pointed at me
when there were no leaves left to speak of.

Inside my son stuttered. Something
about the dog wasn't right.

She didn't flinch when I touched her.
Was it possible, in this light,
that she was simply resting on the rug?

Sometime later scattered pieces interlocked,
each part the blueprint of a better truth
seen in better light,

                    a fiction we need,
at least for the hours before light outside
appears to make the changes on its own.

Prayer

A van on the street has a sign that says *Pray*.
      A voice calls out.
I hear my son's name,
      but I can't see in
the smoked-glass windows.
      I realize it's Eoin,
the brother of Finnian, my son's friend.
      Eoin wanders if you stop watching,
then he's gone.

I love Finn's angel face
      made for the smile he wears—
Eoin always looks away,
      looks away, his face flushed
when no one understands
      what he's saying. He doesn't know
he lives in my heart, or why
      when the van drives away
I can't pray to the blind, listless heavens.

Interior Monologue of a Person

In a field, now lightly covered
with the soft hair of a season's new grass,

prisoners given spades are forbidden
to speak the words:

> *body, person, flesh, skin*

They were to call us "figures"—:
"puppets," "blocks of wood."

The day they uncovered me,
I rested against a banker from Lodz.

A young girl's cheekbone
received my hand for eternity.

You can still see where the officer–physician
took a scalpel to the light

camouflage of the skin
to find what was impure in me.

Invisible strings jerk my limbs
and I am

> listening for syllables of a name.

Stevens in New Haven

So late in the day's light, the poet
imagined that he was surrounded
by people, the poor at rest,
and happy because a man of reality
had come to help them live their lives.

He arranged to have them see
what he had seen: the plain grandeur
of the ordinary evening
without gilt-edged haloes,
or unnecessary wings.

They did not know they could complete
the translation he was winging toward,
that it was possible, it seemed,
to have grown all mind
and, together, see the solitary earth.

The Hours Turning

Mossy beards hang
  from a waterwheel
turning slowly in the heat

where the water of the canal
  runs through
the vacant square.

At the café I'm the only one,
  thinking nothing,
watching the turning wheel,

a beer cool in my hand,
  the only distraction
two girls, sisters, with the same red hair.

They've been walking up and down,
  staring at me as they pass.
I could measure time by them,

it seems so long I've been sitting there.
  They stop a moment,
take my picture with an old camera,

and this time
  before they walk away
I want to ask just who they think I am.

Spies

The women at the market in Bonnieux
were our neighbors in the orange house
on Rue Elzear Pin. It didn't matter
that their husbands were with the National Front,
or that they packed our groceries roughly—
they never talked to us, never leaned
over the wall bordering the yards.
We shared the same high perch
above the Luberon. The landscape said to gaze
if we wanted but don't touch, like these women
who waited for us to take our hands
from the fruit in their perfect bins.
We didn't hold anything against them.
We hadn't come to see the nakedness of the land,
but we were trespassers speaking tongues.

The Lamps

Christian women in the city of Goult
sit in the shade of old trees on old walls
happy that day-tourists bypass these stones.
They see three wandering Jews
at the gate of their impeccable gardens,
and they prepare a meal for us, the baby
restless in his chair. They don't care who we are.
They've seen hungry families before.
We leave this sanctuary to go back
to our perch across the valley
where they can see us turn off our lamps,
go to bed with the doors open
and stare at their one last light, pretending
it's for us, that we haven't gone too far.

The View

An artist in Cucuron drew women
with their legs slightly parted,
each caught unaware
of how he had seen them.
I gazed at the paintings in a window
across from a café when three girls,
dressed to find something unusual,
walked into the view. I saw their eyes
look down as their waiter brought them drinks
and said for them, *Bonjour Monsieur,*
Merci Monsieur, demonstrating the smile
he wanted returned to him.
My waitress took my glass, showed me her back
as she walked inside, wanting to be seen.

No Better Claim

Just south of Les Baux you see Van Gogh
didn't distort the view,
the landscape still a stubble of leafless sticks
poking through the hills, which must be why
he preferred the curled tips of cypresses
brushing against the stars, yellow light
on the yellow flowers, or the blue evenings,
green clouds swirling in a glass
on a table under a red lamp
where dark, unaccommodating men
eye women burning with violet intensity.
In the white morning you can't find
his colors. They'd all been taken—
or had no better frame for the impossible sun
than the small window of our indifferent train.

Le Ghetto

Poncet descended on the valley sheltering Pézenas,
orange light on the orange rock
blinding him with each turn toward the city.

His darker nature drew him to a cul-de-sac
beyond the sun's reach.
Whisper, rabbi: this had been the Rue Juiveries.

He sees a tower. He sees a woman bathing
in the *mikveh* in a tower above the street.

The knight-historian had forgotten
the blood stirring in him, having believed
he'd found in solitude desire's perfect form.

The woman does not avert her eyes.
She does not cover her breast—

it is he who turns away
and sees blood running in the gutter,
a butcher slaughtering blesséd meat.

III.

Evidence of Things Unseen

Fontaine-de-Vaucluse

Up and down the walk, bending with the river,
the crowd clattered and slapped,
looking for images to match what was in their books.

I was beneath them on the bank of the Sorgue,
staring at water so translucent—
no depths out of eye's reach.

                  A mile up the path
Jacques Cousteau sent an electric eye
a thousand feet down
to find the source of the resurgent spring.
The probe exploded before it reached the sandy bed
without disturbing the quiet pool

                  where Petrarch had a vision,
real as his own breath,
and in his seclusion must have known
why the eye is a sad traveler.

The Gardener

On mild days, the ailing cypress in Bonnieux
curled like a plume against the mountain.

The wind made sounds of acceptance.
The mountain barely moved.

His mind took in the same light
that released rigid crows from Van Gogh's eyes.

When the mistral started to blow back
the ranks of trees and reveal the roots
and aeries, hollows, lairs, the fallen boughs

of the shivering mountain, it sang in the limbs.
It sang in his lover's thighs.

The Rabbis

They were blessed with nothing,
their eyes purged of ideas.

When the wind scourged the Alpilles,
no leaf turned a silvery back to the heavens.

Ploughed fields were psalms offering fruit,
perfect in number, weight, and measure,

each vineyard a page that moved
the mind across the distance in an instant.

Nothing chased the sun, who was not fleeing
across her own golden path

but glittering in the evening
when a lover slipped from her gown
and called me to return to Provence.

Association for the Recovery of Historical Memory

We may find *tu abuelo* among the graves
of the *desaparecidos*, her father said,
near the edge of the hole they were digging.

The girl collected bullets and tibias.
Some skeletons still wore *albarcas*,
hard-soled shoes made from old car tires.

She saw tough green roots binding the bones,
poking through a cranium, and red dirt
dampened by the rain.

They say when Lorca heard the artillery
he hid under a bed. For many years
he'd been practicing his death.

Her father had woken her early that morning.
She was stirring from a cave of sleep
when he gently drew the blankets from her head.

Letter to Prague, 1948

Dear City,
for some who lost your steeples,
gray pavers, soft loam,
the afternoon of Jerusalem
meant too much light,
the gold promise at the desert's horizon
a disarming radiance.

I regret to tell you of one who kicked over
a wooden chair.

Once on the road to Ashkelon
an Arab picked me up,
his hands waving wildly as he drove.
He tried to sell me his daughter.
Her fingers tangled my dark hair.
I was a displaced person
hurtling through a madness of sand.

           She is gone now—:
my mother who refused
to speak this language I sing
in the wilderness,
my mouth full of stones.

House of Alms

for J.V. Cunningham

I've wasted time with the best of them,
save perhaps that do-nothing Cunningham,
who understood nothing so well
as a knowing self in solitude can.

I seek a little winter love in the dark-lit
corners of his house, that book of alms
where I've looked into his glass
in the mirror of a Waltham bar at the last call.

The evening runs down a cold artery,
home to where the lines have been mined,
and don't I know how I'm no kid anymore
when I hear in the snow how my voice falls.

Self-Portrait

Here in a room, say with pale yellow walls,
sound rising up, a television left on
two floors below, and a child
talking as a mother leans
to rinse soap from his hair, background
chatter is the soundtrack of memory,
not its false twin nostalgia—no ache
to return home. That's art. It's still warm here.
There are no flowers floating in a bowl,
no fruit that one eats, too smooth, like the way
we remember their faces after people leave,
how they recede into the perfect,
that kind of beauty, death, but I am a portrait
that does not sit still in my unpainted chair.

Jupiter & Antiope

In Jupiter Rembrandt saw a satyr
relishing a sleeping figure.

Look! She snores. Her breasts begin to quiver.
The god feels it in his horns.

A cartoon drawn densely dark,
more real than color,

the chiaroscuro pure desire,
nothing noble, and, for that, more real.

It is enough to move professors
to theorize on the bourgeoisie,

then, sated, go to bed in the suburbs.
The only end of desire

is the mind's say-so, a clamp fixed on a vein,
and still Jupiter crouches

by the sleeping Antiope. Still she dreams
of a god's golden body.

Ruin

Stone by stone, perched high above the village,
I was restoring de Sade's castle.
I had purchased it forty years ago
to bring order to the wreckage,
but never finished, or simply couldn't
close off the jagged walls edging the sky.
Hard to say whether I'd been undone
by the Marquis' madness, a solitary monk,
gatekeeper of echoes and ecstatic voices.

Pressure

Shucking quahogs was simple
when I could get the knife in
and catch the muscle cleanly,
scrape the shell to separate
the meat, flip pink side over,
flick the shell in the barrel,
though I seldom felt the blade's
pressure. I'd slit the belly
open where the clam's green gut
showed everything that went wrong
before I doctored it up—
but there was no remedy
for dull knife slips in the flesh
of my hand beneath the thumb
where I'd slice myself open
like an unprotected clam.
It was ruining my hands.
The boss knew I didn't have
to do this for my living
and waited for me to quit,
baited me, making me stand
on the bar to clean the grease
from the lamps and take barrels
weighted down with the day's shells.
No one ever poured a drink
until I dragged myself back.
Beer was good when we lingered
there, the only ones who could
no longer smell the liquor
of the fish all over us.

The Bioluminescent Bay

Who knows the shape it has to take, or time
to reach the privacy of single mind,
like the top room of this house,
eaves conforming to the outside,
one window open just enough
to see the sky, the tips of trees, fractions
of clouds taking years to pass, the landscape
waiting for the mind to sit still, go through
its paces, walk off pains, then row plainly
with oars across a glassy bay
hugged by arms of mangroves,
water swarming with luminous beings
who cooperate with the body's edges
swimming at night.

The Blue Men of Provence

White light sharpens the crags,
      gargoyles looking over the valley
where blue men among the sunflowers
      lift their drooping heads.
See it travel the brass curves—
      A National Front marching band!
The notes cajole people tired of the sun.
      They watch the mayor take the stand,
raise his glass of *vin ordinaire*.
      He silences the snares with a swift hand
as I sit, warm air filling the space
      of my heart, and stare
at the mountain's crown until the sun sets
      and the white rock melts like snow.

Poem

God of grime
and the dirty feet
of common people
kneeling before her
in a Loreto doorway
(the weight of the child
makes the Madonna's shoulders ache),
what would you have us see?

A Cemetery Affair

The oldest cemetery in use in Europe...was deeded to the *Juifs du Pape*, Jews who lived in Carpentras under the protection of the Avignon popes....In 1990, a group of people scaled the cemetery wall, toppled thirty-four gravestones, and dug up the grave of an old Jewish rug merchant named Felix Germon, who had died, peacefully, that April.

I know your name, Felix Germon,
and know that you may not speak to me.
So begins what may turn out to be sin
if I disturb the garden cemetery
deeded to the Jews of Carpentras,
where you were unearthed before a star
was sewn into your skin.

I've seen the yellow star in the clothing
of those who wore it while they lived
and went about their way before it sank
into the flesh. I see a tilted slab,
a sign hanging from your neck—:
de la part de ses voisins, it says,
taken from another grave, out of context.

And the evening took silent hold of me
to hear the stitching, the work of quiet fingering.
Did he lean his hand against you
to ease the strain of the meticulous task?
I hear the creak of upturned stone,
smell the earth's breath as you are exhumed,
and wonder why this night, no different
from other nights, makes me afraid
to leave my son sleeping in a room
where stars we've strewn across the ceiling
begin to lose light.

It wasn't hard for the Catholics of Carpentras
to climb over the garden wall
when they courted *chez les Juifs,*
a cemetery affair they used to call it,
as they lay down together in the uncut grass
next to the wild oaks surrounding the burial plots
of the *Juifs du Pape,* the dead who waited
in caskets with holes drilled in
to let their bodies return to earth.

As it rains, a few old Jews lock the gate
while the summer darkens Carpentras.
My son has night fears, sees twins in his sleep
identical as they cleave, and he dreams
he's home only to wake in a strange room.
In the small yard of this house we've taken
a patch of grass is coming in despite a drought
that's lasted weeks. It rains across the peaks
where lightning strikes Mont Ventoux.

And I tend someone else's garden,
watch the water splash from side to side
and catch the light at the edge of the stones
giving proof of an essence that can't be grasped.
My son sees the flash and calls me in.

The luxuriance of your untended garden
throws shadows on the broken stones
near your mound of upturned earth.
Vines tighten their grip around the trees
until they have no choice but to cooperate
with their own end. I see a Catholic girl
on the Paris streets, your wife who said,
He pleased me—what could I do but keep him
from the boxcars when they left Drancy?

I've seen the multitudes of stars
and one made of skin,
a cold shroud of earth around me.
Are you cold where you are?
What is the seal upon thine arm?
A bracelet of hair gently twined there.
Could one be sufficient to repair the song?
May one star sing if the rest can't be heard?
Where were you when the universe was made?

I was with my son to ease his sleep,
not afraid of death for those who enter
uninitiated and lose themselves
in an ecstasy that figures the union
                of the cherubim.
I can't speculate on an unknown name,
though yours, Felix, is the fortunate pain
that lifts a cloak from one who's freed
and this night has again begun to sing.

The Empty Appeal of the Pyrenees

Beneath the mountain's surface,
ocher veins reveal
what the landscape hides,
crickets the color of dust
flashing blue and red
when their wings part,
the rusty tears
of a white Christ,
when rain finally comes,
trickling from his eyes.
To see them takes time—:
to still the self,
to find the right word.

Catch & Release

I.
I wasn't there to prevent you
from jamming your fingers
on a window's separating panes.

If only you'd remember the catch on the frame.
The release requires three hands:
two to push up, one to press gently.

The river at the end of the street
fills with hungry blues. You're landlocked.
You smell the salt climbing the breeze.

I wonder, close to the water,
what still keeps you a helpless hidden fish.

II.
You hate when I pause after you call me,
but I was thinking

about the shavings of cheese we left on the table,
about what was in the talon of the hawk
perched on a white van today.

Why should anything matter
in a waking dream?

The hawk wasn't a hawk,
a mouse not merely in the claw,
and our table was clean after we left here.

III.
Last night I held a lamp over our room
strewn with clothes.

I waited for the curtains to billow,
raise them with the August air,
and thought, why would angels want us here?

It's always my last task to draw the shades,
though I've made an art of delaying.

The mind wants to wait but the body paces floors,
the last of the day in their pine.

ABOUT THE AUTHOR

Richard Wollman was born in New York and educated at Brandeis University. He received a doctorate from Columbia University in 1994. He is Associate Professor of English and Co-Director of the Zora Neale Hurston Literary Center at Simmons College. He lives in Newburyport, Massachusetts.